THE HOLY WAR
Jihad

LESEA PUBLISHING, INC.
P.O. Box 12
South Bend, IN 46624

OTHER WORKS BY THE SAME AUTHOR...

Living Free
Miracles Don't Just Happen
Demons The Answer Book
Run With The Vision
Ecstasy
Cup Of Life
The Face Of Jesus
The True Story Of Clarita Villanueva
Destroying Your Deadliest Enemy
Seven Ways Jesus Healed The People
JIHAD The Holy War

For Additional Information And Your Free Catalog
Write Today To:

Box 12, Dept. B
South Bend, IN 46624

Jihad

THE HOLY WAR

THE DESTINY OF THE MOSLEM WORLD

by

DR. LESTER SUMRALL

President, Lester Sumrall Evangelistic Association, Inc.

Jihad

Library of Congress Catalog Card Number

80-52479

First printing, July 1980
Second printing, October 1980

Printed in the United States of America

FOREWORD

JIHAD
THE HOLY WAR

When the Ayatollah Khomeini, the religious and political revolutionary of Iran, donated to Arafat, the leader of the P.L.O. (Palestine Liberation Organization) hundreds of millions of dollars to engage Israel in battle, it revealed that the deposed Shah of Iran was not the only rich man in the country.

Khomeini, as an Imman, a Moslem religious leader, possesses tremendous wealth in land and gold.

More important, the millions of dollars given to support Arafat revealed that the holding of American hostages in Iran was JIHAD, the ancient Arabian declaration of Holy War.

Jerusalem is the center and heart-beat of the Middle East crisis. The JIHAD hopes to draw the whole world into this bloody vortex of prophetical warfare.

IRAN, having 4000 years of recorded history is the best vantage point to observe history and the ultimate destiny of the peoples of the region as revealed in the world's most reliable textbook — the Bible.

To be ignorant of the religious convictions of the Ayatollah Khomeini is dangerous, religiously, economically, and politically.

DEDICATION

This volume is dedicated to those pioneers of Christian television who braved the O. and O. dangers of hardships of a new frontier. They will bring millions to Christ in this generation.

ACKNOWLEDGEMENTS

I wish to thank Louise Sumrall my wife, and Billye Brim for their invaluable contributions to this book of history and prophecy.

CONTENTS

INTRODUCTION

THE evidence is overwhelming!

Jesus is coming again!

The Iran Crisis is one more powerful sign pointing the way.

The Russian Bear sits poised like a black widow spider — ready to pounce upon its unsuspecting prey. The prize — little Israel. Three million plus Jews are surrounded by more than 100 million hostile Arabs, most of them supported with Russian fire power. God's hook is set in the Russian jaw — she is being irresistibly drawn to that inevitable rendezvous where she shall be judged and most of her military power annihilated.

Dr. Sumrall has documented from the prophetic Word of God Iran's unique role in God's plan of the ages and the final drama of this Dispensation.

Now is the time for the church and body of Christ to arise and reap the final harvest of immortal souls.

Now is the time to win our lost loved ones and neighbors. It will never be easier — God's

Holy Spirit is active and moving in the world! Joel's prophecy is being fulfilled. The Spirit is falling in conviction upon all flesh. Body of Christ, let's get the job done now so that Jesus can return! Jesus said:

" And when these things begin to come to pass, then look up, and lift up your heads, for your redemption draweth nigh." Luke 21:28

I commend this exciting new book and Dr. Sumrall to you knowing that you will be blessed and inspired to do your part in bringing back the King!

Paul F. Crouch, President
TRINITY BROADCASTING NETWORK
Los Angeles, California

Chapter 1
ELAM:
Grandson of Noah, Father of Iran

Iran shocked the world and commanded the attention of its newspaper headlines and broadcast bulletins when it captured the embassy of one of the world's most powerful nations on November 4, 1979 and took hostage sixty-three citizens of the "land of the free."

Knowledgeable students of Bible prophecy were the least surprised at that terrible intrusion. They had been watching for a move from this ancient land. For neither modern Iran, nor the Islamic world, can escape their past history or future destiny.

You're not a student of Bible prophecy, you

say? How can you know what to expect from Iran and the Moslem world?

My purpose in writing this book is to help you to know. Trace with me the history of Iran through the pages of the Bible. It is not difficult to do. It's not hidden. It's not beyond your grasp. In fact, you will be fascinated at how your understanding of current world events widens in the light of God's Holy Word.

IRAN: An Ancient Land

Iran — called Persia until 1935 when it was renamed by its then Shah — has nearly four thousand years of recorded and known history.

The story begins with Noah's grandson, Elam.

But let's go back to the beginning — the beginning of man.

Adam, the first human, knew God on a very personal, one-to-one basis. Adam walked and talked with God. Adam knew how to worship the "Elohim" God in an acceptable manner. But Adam fell and mankind with him. This was approximately six thousand years ago.

Some two thousand years after the Eden catastrophe, only Noah knew God on a one-to-one basis. He preached and prepared for a hundred years for the deluge God told him would cover the earth. No one, outside his family, believed.

What a treasure was carried in the Ark that saved them! It was mankind's knowledge of God.

At this point in time, Noah and his family were the only Homo sapiens on the planet earth. They knew the true God and worshiped Him.

Noah's sons — Shem, Ham, and Japheth — left the Ark with their parents with a tremendous respect for the living God and divine order. They heard the voice of God and witnessed the birth of the rainbow — God's promise not to destroy the earth again with water. They stood at Noah's altar with heads bowed as the God of the universe promised there would never be another world-wide flood. They heard God's promise of perpetual seedtime and harvest.

Shem, Ham, and Japheth also remembered how wickedly the people lived who were destroyed by the flood.

What a tremendous memory bank! What knowledge to pass on from these three fathers to their offspring — **the entire world's population!**

Iran and Early Biblical History

Bible geneology after the flood is found in Genesis chapters 10 and 11.

To Shem — Noah's son — Elam, Asshur, Arphaxad, Lud, and Aram were born (Gen. 10:22).

Elam became a tribe, built cities, ultimately vanquished Babylon, and became the Persian empire. Iran's history is traceable through Elam.

Elam was at least one year older than his brother, Arphaxad. It is in Arphaxad's line that we find Abraham only ten generations from Noah's flood.

1. Shem. "Noah begat three sons, Shem, Ham, and Japheth" (Gen. 6:10).

2. Arphaxad. "Shem was an hundred years

old, and begat Arphaxad two years after the flood" (Gen. 11:10).

3. Salah. "And Arphaxad lived five and thirty years, and begat Salah" (v. 12).

4. Eber. "And Salah lived thirty years, and begat Eber" (v. 14).

5. Peleg. "And Eber lived four and thirty years, and begat Peleg" (v. 16).

6. Reu. "and Peleg lived thirty years, and begat Reu" (v. 18).

7. Serug. "And Reu lived two and thirty years, and begat Serug" (v. 20).

8. Nahor. "And Serug lived thirty years, and begat Nahor" (v. 22).

9. Terah. "And Nahor lived nine and twenty years, and begat Terah" (v. 24).

10. Abram (Abraham). "And Terah lived seventy years, and begat Abram, Nahor, and Haran" (v. 26).

During these ten generations, many left the truth of God. Some began to serve idols.

These relatively few years witnessed the "Tower of Babel" and the dispersion of the nations by language (Gen. 11:3-9). In order for God to preserve the promised Seed of the woman and fulfil His prophecy given at the

Garden of Eden (Gen. 3:15), He had to separate men — evil from good. God did this by confusion of language at Babel.

These years also witnessed, in the days of Peleg, the division of the earth from one land mass into continents and islands (Gen. 10:25). God again separated the good, God-fearing people from the rest of mankind. This was His means of bringing the world a Savior, Jesus Christ.

Less than four hundred years after the flood, God spoke to Abram on a one-to-one basis and told him to leave Ur of the Chaldees — the area where the Assyrian, the Babylonian, and Persian empires would later spring up.

It was Elamite raids that destroyed Ur about 1950 BC.

Chapter 2
Father Abraham Fights Iran

It was Jehovah God who spoke to Abraham and caused him to leave Ur of the Chaldees, a place where many had become worshipers of idols and demon spirits — the general area which would become Elam and Persia and Iran.

The story of the flood had now passed through ten generations.

Now don't look at the Bible with vast distances. I hold in my experience knowledge of five generations. I remember my grandfather well; I know my grandchildren well. Some people remember great grandparents and live to know great grandchildren.

In only ten generations after Noah, in order

to separate evil from good, God demanded Abraham to depart from Ur of the Chaldees.

Jehovah's divine guidance led him north to Haran across the desert into Canaan which was to become his homeland and the "Promised Land" to him and his seed after him.

In the land of Canaan Abraham continued to serve the true God of Noah and Adam.

He had amazing increase in his possessions. *"Abram was very rich in cattle, in silver, and in gold"* (Gen. 13:2).

And so was his nephew, Lot, whom he had brought along with him. *"and Lot also, which went with Abram, had flocks, and herds, and tents. And the land was not able to bear them, that they might dwell together: for their substance was great, so that they could not dwell together"* (Gen. 13:5,6).

The two could no longer live within the same grazing space for their cattle. They had to separate. But the land was great before them. Abraham gave Lot his choice saying, *"If thou wilt take the left hand, then I will go to the right; or if thou depart to the right hand, then I will go to the left"* (v. 9).

Lot chose the well-watered plain of Jordan.

Journeying eastward he pitched his tent toward the city of Sodom where there was exceeding sin. Eventually he moved into that wicked city and became an official in the city gate of Sodom.

Several years after Lot left Abraham, the city state of Sodom was beseiged and captured by the kings of the Fertile Crescent.

"It came to pass in the days of Amraphel king of Shinar, Arioch king of Ellasar, Chedorlaomer king of Elam, and Tical king of nations; that these made war with Bera king of Sodom, and with Birsha king of Gomorrah, Shinab king of Admah, and Shemeber king of Zeboiim, and the king of Bela, which is Zoar. All these were joined together in the vale of Siddim, which is the salt sea" (Gen. 14:1-3).

In this first recorded war in the Bible, we note Chedorlaomer, king of Elam. He was the leader of a coalition of kings from the same area Abraham had departed at God's command.

For twelve years the five principal cities in the Jordan plain, including Sodom and Gomorrah, had been made to serve Chedorlaomer and pay him tribute.

In the thirteenth year, the cities of the plain rebelled.

In the fourteenth year, the confederacy of kings headed up by the king of Elam came to put down the insurrection.

They smote Sodom and Gomorrah and took all their goods, their victuals, and many of their people as hostages. (Iran has been taking hostages for a long time.) Among their captives was Abraham's brother's son, Lot.

Word of the capture reached Abraham. Someone who escaped the battle came with the news to Mamre where Abraham dwelled.

Abraham took three hundred and eighteen servants of his own house, armed them, and pursued the invading kings from Hebron in the south, through the hills of Judea, across Megiddo, up through the hills of Galilee, to Dan where he overtook them. A long pursuit!

Abraham divided his band and attacked by night. Then he chased the kings to Hobnah, north of Damascus, where he completely destroyed them.

He destroyed the powers of Persia in one night!

Genesis 14:17 tells how the king of Sodom came out to meet Abraham *"after his return from the slaughter of Chedorlaomer and of the kings that were with him.''*

Abraham brought Sodom's riches back to them and gave his nephew, Lot, his life.

Within a few years time, Abraham had to fight the people of Elam where he had come from as a young man. God gave him power over the kings from his homeland. This is witnessed by Melchizedek's blessing when he met Abraham upon his return from the victory.

"And Melchizedek king of Salem brought forth bread and wine: and he was the priest of the most high God. And he blessed him, and said, Blessed be Abram of the most high God, possessor of heaven and earth: And blessed be the most high God, which hath delivered thine enemies into thy hand. And he gave him tithes of all'' (Gen. 14:18-20).

The first step into biblical history for Iran was when it faced the man of God, Abraham, and its king, Chedolaomer, was destroyed.

Chapter 3
Iran and Empire

Permit me to grasp your spirit so that we can walk together in the prophetical truth which will bring you an understanding of the times. For it is only through the Bible that anyone can understand them.

More than twenty-five hundred years ago God spoke to a man named Daniel in visions and dreams and showed him empires unborn. History verifies the fact that this man prophesied the rise and fall of empires. Today you can see the blueprint of the future through this man of God named Daniel.

Daniel, a young prince of Judah, was carried off into captivity with other children of Israel by Nebuchadnezzar king of Babylon. There he was chosen, with other outstanding young captives, to be trained in the king's college for three years.

Daniel purposed in his heart to obey the living God. He would not defile himself with the king's meat or wine. Three fellow captives joined him.

God gave them favor and elevated them to high positions in the empire.

"As for these four children, God gave them knowledge and skill in all learning and wisdom: and Daniel had understanding in visions and dreams. Now at the end of the days that the king had said he should bring them in, then the prince of the eunuchs brought them in before Nebuchadnezzar. And the king communed with them; and among them all was found none like Daniel, Hananiah, Mishael, and Azariah: therefore stood they before the king. And in all matters of wisdom and understanding, that the king inquired of them, he found them ten times better than all the magicians and astrologers that were in all his realm" (Dan. 1:17-20).

First Prophetic Picture of Iran: Silver

Daniel, through supernatural power, saw the

entire scope of world empires — but only those empires prophetically involved with Christ — in three revelations.

The first revelation initally came as a dream to the worldly king, Nebuchadnezzar (Dan. 2:1-18).

The dream and its interpretation were revealed unto Daniel in a night vision (Dan. 1:19).

Daniel said, in the presence of the king, *"There is a God in heaven that revealeth secrets, and maketh known to the king Nebuchadnezzar what shall be in the latter days"* (Dan. 1:28).

Most believers know that we are in "the latter days."

First, Daniel told the king the dream. *"Thou, O king, sawest, and behold a great image. This great image, whose brightness was excellent, stood before thee; and the form thereof was terrible.*

"This image's head was of fine gold, his breast and his arms of silver, his belly and his thighs of brass, his legs of iron, his feet part of iron and part of clay.

"Thou sawest till that a stone was cut out without hands, which smote the image upon his feet that were of iron and clay, and brake them to pieces" (Dan. 2:31-34).

JIHAD

BABYLONIAN EMPIRE
Lion — Daniel 7:4

"Thou art the head of gold."
Dan. 2:38

GOLD

MEDO-PERSIAN EMPIRE
Bear — Daniel 7:5

"After thee shall arise another
kingdom inferior to thee."
Dan. 2:39

SILVER

GRECIAN EMPIRE
Leopard — Daniel 7:6

"Another third kingdom of
brass which shall bear rule
over all the earth."
Dan. 2:39b

BRASS

ROMAN EMPIRE
Monstrous Beast
Daniel 7:8,9

Teeth of Iron — Rule
Ten Horns — Kings
Little Horn — Antichrist

"And the fourth kingdom
shall be strong as iron."
Dan. 2:40

IRON

**IRON AND
CLAY**

The Stone
Dan. 2:34-45

Western World   Eastern World

Then Daniel gave the king the interpretation. God revealed through Daniel that the great metallic colossus foretold the future of mankind.

The metallic man revealed four great prophetic world empires — the entire period of Gentile supremacy in the world — until the end of time.

Gold — Babylonian Empire *"Thou, O king, art a king of kings: for the God of heaven hath given thee a kingdom, power, and strength, and glory. And wheresoever the children of men dwell, the beasts of the field and the fowls of the heaven hath he given into thine hand, and hath made thee ruler over them all. Thou art this head of gold"* (Dan. 2:37, 38). The golden empire of the centuries was Babylon — none ever rose such as it. Babylon fell to the Persians in 539 BC.

Silver — Medo-Persian Empire *"After thee shall arise another kingdom inferior to thee . . ."* (Dan.2:39). Our first prophetic picture of Iran — shoulders, arms, and chest of silver. The empire indeed had two arms — the Medes and the Persians. They were together, members of the same family. The Persians superseded the Medes and dominated the kingdom.

Brass — Grecian Empire *" . . . and another third kingdom of brass, which shall bear rule over all the earth"* (Dan. 2:39). This kingdom began with Alexander the Great and was later controlled by four army generals. In 334 BC Alexander set about liberating Greece from Persian control and launching the sweeping campaign which resulted in a new empire.

Iron (Clay and Iron) — Roman Empire *"And the fourth kingdom shall be strong as iron"* (Dan. 2:40). The Roman empire arose two hundred years before Christ. It was seen first divided into two — the legs — fulfilled in the Eastern and Western Roman empires. Then it was seen divided into ten — the toes (the feet and toes were clay and iron) — this is the federation of nations under one head, the antichrist, which exists at the end of the present age.

Second Prophetic Picture of Iran: The Bear

King Nebuchadnezzar's vision of the metallic man gave the imposing outward glory of the destiny of empires. God revealed their natures in a vision given to Daniel forty-eight years later.

"In the first year of Belshazzar king of Babylon Daniel had a dream and visions of his head upon his bed . . . Daniel spake and said, I saw in my vision by night, and, behold, the four winds of the heaven strove upon the great sea" (Dan. 7:1,2).

This reveals the movement of strength and might upon multitudes of people. In God's Word "the sea" is always multitudes of people. Daniel saw the furious empires of the world moving like tempestuous winds upon a stormy sea.

"And four great beasts came up from the sea (again the sea of people), *diverse one from another"* (v. 3). Every empire in history has been different from all others.

"The first was like a lion, and had eagle's wings . . ." (v. 4). This kingdom is the same as the golden head. It is now described as a lion. As gold is the finest of metals, so the lion is the strongest of beasts. Babylon was a much greater nation than many modern people realize. The lion had eagle's wings. This signifies the speed in which it moved to conquer the world and

carry out its own wishes. Great strength and velocity symbolized Babylon.

Our special interest in this book is the second empire.

"And behold another beast, a second, like to a bear, and it raised up itself on one side, and it had three ribs in the mouth of it between the teeth of it: and they said thus unto it, Arise, devour much flesh" (v. 5).

In Daniel's vision Persia was a bear.

The Medes and the Persians were one army together — but Persia raised itself up on one side and destroyed the Medes. Thus it became solely the Persian empire.

The three ribs in the bear's mouth signify three major nations it had conquered — Media, Lydia, and Babylon. All were conquered by Persia. Persia boasted that she ruled 127 provinces from India to Egypt.

All the great empires were ruthless and killed many. "Much flesh devoured" speaks of the terrible violence and quick destruction exacted upon this empire's enemies. The bear is a vicious predator, a killer. In like manner, Persia was a devourer of nations.

"After this I beheld, and lo another, like a leopard, which had upon the back of it four wings of a fowl; the beast had also four heads; and dominion was given to it" (v. 7).

The Grecian empire was known for its great speed, for its hiding, and for its killing. God likened it unto a leopard with four wings and four heads.

"After this I saw in the night visions, and behold a fourth beast, dreadful and terrible, and strong exceedingly; and it had great iron teeth: it devoured and brake in pieces, and stamped the residue with the feet of it: and it was diverse from all the beasts that were before it; and it had ten horns" (v 7).

The fourth beast was unlike any other beast. It was the Roman empire. In the end it was to have ten horns, representing ten nations, and a little horn which ultimately produces the antichrist who will stand up before Christ and fight against him at the end of time.

Third Prophetic Picture of Iran: Ram

Two years after the vision recorded in Daniel

chapter 7, the Lord gave Daniel a further vision of empires. This vision came to him in the third year of Belshazzar (553 BC).

Daniel says something very strange as he begins to relate it, *"I saw in a vision; and it came to pass, when I saw, that I was at Shushan in the palace, which is in the province of Elam; and I saw in a vision, and I was by the river of Ulai"* (Dan. 8:2).

We already know the province of Elam becomes Persia and then Iran. Shushan is its Persian capital and the structure of the royal palace. The royal city was known as "Shushan the palace." The business and residential area was known as "Shushan the city." Daniel saw that world power was to be transferred to the kingdom of Persia. This would be fulfilled fourteen years later in 539 BC.

"Then I lifted up mine eyes, and saw, and, behold, there stood before the river a ram which had two horns: and the two horns were high; but one was higher than the other, and the higher came up last" (v. 3).

God gave Daniel the interpretation of the ram in verse 20: *"The ram which thou sawest having two horns are the kings of Media and Persia."*

The two horns represent the twin nations of

the Medes and the Persians in the beginning. Then one horn lifted itself up higher than the other and the Persians destroyed the Medes and became sole rulers of the empire.

"I saw the ram pushing westward, and northward, and southward . . ." (v. 4). The ram's thrust of power was westward toward Israel and the Mediterranean Sea, northward toward Russia and Turkey, and southward toward Africa. Persia boasted that all existing armies were defeated and her rule was over one hundred twenty-seven provinces with a prince ruling each province.

Daniel also saw the fall of the Persian empire. He tells of a great "he goat" coming from the west (v. 5). Greece is in the west. The he goat did not touch the ground. He moved with such velocity and power and speed, he ran into the ram which was Persia — smote him, broke his horns, cast him to the ground and stomped upon him.

"Therefore the he goat waxed very great . . ." (v. 8). The Grecian empire began to rule the world.

. . .*"and when he was strong, the great horn was broken; and for it came up four notable ones toward the four winds of heaven"* (v. 8). Alexander the

Great died at a very young age. Four generals ruled, dividing his kingdom.

History Before It Happens

These prophecies by the prophet Daniel became an accurate record of history which was to come.

One of the proofs that God is God is that many years before these empires came into power, God through his servants revealed their likeness, their strength, their rise and their fall, and the one that would succeed them — even unto the last empire which has to do with the Stone which was cut out of the mountain without hands. More about this later.

Chapter 4
The Persian Empire and the Plan of God

It is remarkable that we can follow Noah's grandson, Elam, through the pages of history until his tribe becomes a mighty empire — an empire which blessed the work of God.

The Babylonian empire had conquered Israel, destroying its capital city, Jerusalem — its walls, its gates, its Temple. They robbed the Temple of its treasures and carried them away to Babylon.

The Persian empire returned the captives to their homeland and helped them rebuild their walls, their gates, and their Temple, giving them money and provisions to do so. They returned the vessels of the House of the Lord which Nebuchadnezzar had brought to Babylon (Ezra 1:7-11).

The Books of Ezra, Nehemiah, Esther, Isaiah, Jeremiah, Haggai, Zechariah, and Malachi testify to this. They tell the story of the Persian empire as related to the people through whom God would bring a Savior to the world. They prophesy relating to Iran and its destiny.

Cyrus, king of Persia, founded the Medo-Persian empire. He is the king who returned the Jews to Judea.

Ezra chapter 1 tells his story and declares that it was the Lord who stirred him up to do so.

"Now in the first year of Cyrus king of Persia, that the word of the Lord by the mouth of Jeremiah might be fulfilled, the Lord stirred up the spirit of Cyrus king of Persia, that he made a proclamation throughout all his kingdom, and put it also in writing, saying, Thus saith Cyrus king of Persia, The Lord God of heaven hath given me all the kingdoms of the earth; and he hath charged me to build him an house at Jerusalem, which is in Judah" (Ezra 1:1,2).

It is fascinating that the prophet Isaiah had foretold this — even naming the king —

seventy-six years before (Is. 44:28;45:1,13).

The son of Cyrus, Cambyses, became emperor of Persia at his father's death. He went forth to conquer Egypt and was fantastically successful in putting down rebellion in Egypt. But on his journey home, he died.

An imposter named Pseudo Smerdis grabbed the throne for the emperor was out of the country when he died. He ruled Persia six months before being killed by Darius.

King Darius, after taking the throne, defeated nine kings in nineteen battles. He brought Persia to an unquestionable place of supremacy in the world, putting down all rebellion in the world against it.

The Temple Rebuilt

During the reign of Darius, Jerusalem was a scene of activity between 520 and 515 BC, as the Temple was rebuilt under the prophetic leadership of Haggai and Zechariah.

The Walls Go Up

Nehemiah, a Jew, was cupbearer to the famous Persian king, Artaxerxes. In Nehemiah 1:4 we observe this man in high position to be a man of prayer. His determination was so strong he prayed for four months before appearing before the king to present his cause.

Because of his acceptance by the Persian king, he was commissioned to go to Jerusalem and rebuild the walls and the gates.

The emperor provided Nehemiah with finances and letters to all the governors of the provinces and gave him protection.

The People May Return

Ezra was greatly respected and found favor with Artaxerxes. So much so that the king made this decree: *"I make a decree, that all they of the people of Israel, and of his priests and Levites, in my realm, which are minded of their own freewill to go up to Jerusalem, go with thee"* (Ezra 7:13). This was decreed in 457 BC.

Iran had a very vital part in the rebirth of Israel. What the empire of Babylon had destroyed, the empire of Persia had rebuilt.

When Iran gave sympathy to the Jews and helped them to rebuild, it played a part in the plan of God. For it was through these Jews that a way was being prepared for the eternal King, Jesus, to come.

Chapter 5
Iran and its Jewish Queen

It is amazing how God keeps putting His finger into politics.

He has always had a witness in every empire. When Egypt was the greatest country in the world, Joseph was right there bossing the thing. When Babylon was at the zenith of its power, Daniel was there giving the forecast and the truth for that land. And at the peak of the Persian empire, a Jewish queen came to the throne.

Ahasuerus, son of Darius, had succeeded his father to the throne. This Ahasuerus, or Xerxes, was a militant emperor. He maintained the scope and splendor of the Persian empire and was sucessful in keeping his more restless subjects under control.

45

He ruled from India even unto Ethiopia over one hundred twenty-seven provinces (Esth. 1:1). This is the vastness of the Persian empire.

Under Ahasuerus, an amazing page of history took place in "Shushan the palace" — capital city of the world. All nations brought their gold and silver to this city of world dictatorship. This city is located one hundred fifty miles north of the Persian Gulf east of the Tigris River. The Persians called it Sush then (Sushan is Hebrew) — today it is called Shush.

It was in this city that Queen Esther's divine destiny preserved a nation.

"Shushan the palace" was a city within the city — a royal capital. The story begins with a remarkably long feast that took place there.

"In the third year of his reign, he (Ahasuerus) *made a feast unto all his princes and his servants; the power of Persia and Media, the nobles and princes of the provinces being before him: When he shewed the riches of his glorious kingdom and the honour of his excellent majesty many days, even an hundred and fourscore days"* (Esth. 1:3,4).

How would you like to attend a feast that lasted six months?

When that feast was over, he had another one.

"And when these days were expired, the king made a feast unto all the people that were present in Shushan the palace, both unto great and small, seven days, in the court of the garden of the king's palace" (v. 5).

Those garden courts were fabulously decorated (v. 6).

"And they gave them drink in vessels of gold, (the vessels being diverse one from another,) and royal wine in abundance . . ." (Esth. 1:7).

Everyone had a cup made of gold. Several thousand people and no two cups were alike!

These Persians were exceedingly rich.

It is a sad story, but after the feast and the drunken mess, the king asked Queen Vashti to come forward and show her flesh. She would not. So he banished her.

A search went forth throughout all the provinces for all the fair young virgins to be brought unto Shushan the palace to the house of the women. The maiden who pleased the king would be queen instead of Vashti.

In Shushan the palace there was a certain Jew, Mordecai. He was a great man for he sat in the gate of the capital. This meant he had to do with the discourses of the government. This is where they gave justice and answered the problems of the people.

Mordecai had brought up his uncle's orphaned daughter, Hadassah, that is, Esther. She was fair of form and beautiful.

It came to pass that Esther was chosen by the king as the most beautiful maiden and she became queen of the Persian empire.

Special Delivery

In the Book of Nehemiah it is written that God gave His people *"saviours, who saved them out of the hand of their enemies"* (Neh. 9:27).

In the reign of Esther we have one of these special deliveries. It is one of the most fascinating accounts in history.

A man named Haman — a Hitler of his day — who was a Persian prince and stood next to the emperor, planned the total annihilation of the people of Israel.

The king had promoted Haman and advanced him above all the princes. When Haman rode through the streets he asked that everyone in the king's gate bow before him.

One man at the gate would not bow. That was the Jew Mordecai.

Haman was furious. He asked who the man was and why he would not bow.

They told him it was Mordecai, and that he was a Jew.

So Haman said, "I will destroy all Jews."

He gathered information about the Jews and went before the king. The crux of the matter was this. Haman said, "I want to destroy those people called the Jews. I will pay for it myself." He promised $20 million of his personal funds to finance the job.

What he did not know was, Queen Esther was a Jewess. Esther had not yet revealed her lineage.

When Mordecai learned of Haman's plan to destroy all the Jews in all one hundred twenty-seven provinces, he rushed word to Esther charging her that *"she should go in unto the king, to make supplication unto him, and to make request before him for her people"* (Esth. 4:8).

The law of the land was that if anyone, man or woman, should come unto the king who was not called, they would be put to death — unless the king held out his golden sceptre that the person should live.

Esther had not been called to come unto the king for thirty days.

Mordecai sent these powerful words to Esther, *"Who knoweth whether thou art come to the kingdom for such a time as this?"* (Esth. 4:14).

Queen Esther took her life into her hands and went before the king.

"And it was so, when the king saw Esther the queen standing in the court, that she obtained favour in his sight: and the king held out to Esther the golden sceptre that was in his hand. So Esther drew near, and touched the top of the scepter" (Esth. 5:2).

Esther found favor with the Iranian shah and delivered the people of God.

Haman died for his sins. He was hung on the gallows he had prepared for Mordecai.

The Jews were preserved.

And the empire got to know of the true and living God.

Immortal Peace Day
Related to Iran

At the death of Haman and the salvation of the Jews a great feast was celebrated (Esth. 9:17). It was called the Feast of Purim. To this day it is celebrated by Jews all over the world during the first part of February.

I have personally seen the Israeli children play and march through the streets of Israel on this festive day. The mothers bake small cakes in the shape of a triangle which they give to various people on this special peace day. It is a day of rejoicing.

Chapter 6
Iran and the
Birth of Christ

It is most remarkable how certain nations became biblically oriented where the lineage of the nation can be traced similarly to the lineage of a family.

It is also a lesson to learn that when God becomes involved with a person or a nation they owe certain allegiances to Him.

Also, when light comes across our pathway, we must live up to that light or darkness comes into our lives or into our nation. We see that in the present nation of Iran, who in our time, 1935, was known as Persia, a name which took it back twenty-five hundred years to the time it was called Elam. This nation has had many

opportunities to love God and to serve God —
and it still has opportunities today.

As Iran has been involved in Bible history
from the time of Noah, it will continue to be a
part of Bible prophecy until the Kingdom of
Christ is fulfilled.

Wise Men from Iran

*"Now when Jesus was born in Bethlehem of Judaea
in the days of Herod the king, behold, there came wise
men from the east to Jerusalem, Saying, Where is he
that is born King of the Jews? for we have seen his
star in the east, and are come to worship him"* (Matt.
2:1, 2).

This is one of the most amazing stories in the
Bible. It certainly has to do with the supernatural.

How could they know a king was to be born?
How could they know he was to be king of
the Jews?
How could they be interested in a Jewish
king?
Why was it a star they followed?

Possibly these men were acquainted with the
Torah of the writings of Moses. Maybe they
knew Numbers 24:17, *". . . there shall come a Star*

out of Jacob, and a Sceptre shall rise out of Israel . . ."
If they knew prophecy and loved God, they
would be searching the heavens for such a star.
Certainly they had to be guided supernaturally
in order to arrive at this place at this specific
time in history.

Persian history relates that these men came
from their area, from Elam. It says they were
trained in medicine, natural sciences, and as-
tronomy. Today three Iranian cities make
claims that the kings mentioned in Matthew
were from their city. These are Savaha,
Mahadam, and Razyach.

There are remarkable situations in this story.

One is that they were willing to follow a star
in the heavens that was guiding them — what-
ever that star was.

It is also remarkable that they were willing to
do worship and humble themselves before a
child. They expressly said they had come to
worship him.

It is interesting to see that Joseph and Mary
were no longer in a barn or cow stable. They
were in a house when they were found.

"And when they were come into the house, they saw the young child with Mary his mother, and fell down, and worshipped him: and when they had opened their treasures, they presented unto him gifts; gold, and frankincense, and myrrh" (Matt. 2:11).

It is interesting that the commodities in the open market where money could easily be obtained were gold, frankincense, and myrrh. They opened their treasures and presented these three gifts to Jesus.

This was adequate for support for a great length of time. It could take Mary and Joseph and the Child to Egypt. They could live there comfortably. And they could return to their own home safely.

God could have arranged many other things to help the Lord Jesus to go into Egypt for protection against King Herod who finally destroyed the boy babies 2 years old and younger in Bethlehem. For sure, there were rich people about who could have supplied funds for their escape.

Why would the Lord reach back to the place He had brought Abraham from in the beginning and bring forth these people across the burning deserts to this area? Probably we will not understand the full story until we are in heaven.

Certainly, it links Iran with the Bible story in a most intrinsic way. It reveals that God has an interest in the people of that area. It reveals that the people are willing to find and follow divine revelation. It reveals that they were willing to meet a need which was urgent at that time.

It binds Iran forever with the birth of the Savior of the world. The story of the wise men guarantees that the true story of the Savior of the world was told in the Persian land. For those wise men would not have left Bethlehem until Mary had told all — until Joseph had told all — until the Scriptures from Isaiah were clearly explained how that a virgin would conceive and bear a child.

Chapter 7
Iran at the Birth of the Christian Church

When the Son of God was born on planet earth, He came with direct and explicit instructions to save this planet from its sins. This was brought about through the Jewish nation.

Yet though Christ was born into a Jewish family, it was Iranians who came and brought the money to take them to safety and to support them during their moment of need.

The next great event in history after Christ ascended to heaven was the birth of the Christian Church. Could it be possible that these people of Iran who were connected with the birth of the Savior could also be involved in any way with the birth of the Christian Church?

Possibly the most revolutionary day in history was the day the Church was born. Jesus had already said the gates of hell could not prevail against it!

Jesus has already divided humanity into two sections — they that believe and they that believe not.

Now a mighty force—the Church—came into being! The story is told in Acts chapter 2: *"And when the day of Pentecost was fully come, they were all with one accord in one place. And suddenly there came a sound from heaven as of a rushing mighty wind, and it filled all the house where they were sitting. And there appeared unto them cloven tongues like as of fire, and it sat upon each of them. And they were all filled with the Holy Ghost, and began to speak with other tongues, as the Spirit gave them utterance"* (vv. 1-4).

The day had fully come. The Roman roads were ready for them to travel upon. The ships of the world were ready to carry them across its waves. The arsenals of the Roman empire were ready to protect travelers as they journeyed from continent to continent, from nation to nation. The world was ready. God was ready.

Most intensely interesting is who was there the day the Church was born.

At the initial infilling, there were one hundred twenty people in an upper room in a private home. Mary, the mother of Jesus, was there. She belonged to the royal family. The eleven disciples and apostles who had been with him from the beginning and were the foundation stones of the Christian Church were there. A few others are identified. And beyond this, there were more than 100 whose names or addresses we do not know, but they were among those who made it possible for the Church to be born.

After receiving the Holy Spirit, this ecstatic group flowed out of the Upper Room into the Temple area where there was room for everybody. There they found many openhearted people ready to hear.

"And there were dwelling at Jerusalem Jews, devout men, out of every nation under heaven" (v. 5).

How remarkable that Jews and converts to Judaism from throughout the world were in the Temple area to worship God at this great feast of Pentecost on the day the Church was born!

"Now when this was noised abroad, the multitude came together, and were confounded, because that every man heard them speak in his own language" (v. 6).

This miracle simply astounded them. They were amazed. They marvelled, saying one to another, *"Behold, are not all these which speak Galilaeans? And how hear we every man in our own tongue, wherein we were born? Parthian, and Medes, and Elamites . . ."* (vv. 7-9).

Other nations were named, but we will identify these three named first. The Parthians were from the area called Pars, also called Fars, which is in southern Iran. The Medes were located in central Iran. The Elamites were from southwestern Iran and the capital city of Shushan.

The Iranians were there the day the Church was born!

And they went back home and began to plant the Church in their own area. The Church was planted in Persia. Tradition says that Andrew lived in that area — that Bartholomew was a missionary to Armenia — that Thomas labored in Parthia — and that Jude preached and died in Persia. They had living Apostles.

But Iran is not Christian today; it is Mohammedan.

Why?

Chapter 8
JIHAD: Holy War

Webster's New World Dictionary defines JIHAD: a war by Moslems against unbelievers or enemies of Islam, carried out as a religious duty.

Beyond any doubt, among the shifting sands of the Arabian Peninsula, world destiny is being formed. It is very difficult for America to comprehend the vast importance of what is happening in the Near East at this time.

Iran has made itself the center of JIHAD. Its total population is in a frenzy. Suddenly, again emerges the Persian empire.

America's carnal Christians do not realize that the battles of our time are spiritual. In the whole vast world today, the true issues are spiritual.

To understand JIHAD one must know certain things about Islam. To know those things about Islam, one must know certain things about Mohammed and his times.

The World of Mohammed

When Mohammed came on the scene of human activity, the power of Persia was devastated and gone; a bad memory. The Grecian empire had sunk into decay and was no longer a world power. Even the Roman empire lay at its lowest level in dust and defeat.

The Dark Ages had settled over the Western world. The Bible was locked in the cloistered recesses of monasteries away from the common people. There were no other books. And only 15% of the population could read or write.

After the birth of the Christian Church, the Fertile Crescent enjoyed a great thrust of spiritual growth and of the power of God. Many churches were formed. And the Church grew in a wonderful and delightful way. But during the centuries from the first century to the sixth, the Church lost its emphasis, its zeal, its fervor. It ceased to grow either materially or spiritually.

The world was ripe for a revolutionary religion such as Islam to be born. And from the dusty wastes of Arabia, the people were ready for a prophet, good or bad.

So often when we are not positive to produce the person God wants to lead and guide, the devil will give counterfeits. So many times, the one that God wants is not available because people are not ready for such a one.

Mohammed was born in 570 AD in the city of Mecca, thirty years before the end of the 6th century. He died in 632 AD at sixty-two years of age.

The story of Mohammed is that of a child of misfortune. His father died two months before his birth. His mother died when he was six. He was reared by his grandfather, who died later, and then his uncle, Abu Talib.

Abu was a businessman and a trader. His merchant caravans followed the Fertile Crescent from Iran to Egypt. Mohammed greatly enjoyed following these caravans with his uncle and his nephew, Ali.

At the age of twenty-five, Mohammed was a chief camel driver working for Khadija, a wealthy Jewish widow. Three years later, he married her though she was some twenty years older than he was.

Owning a caravan was like owning a railroad or an airline today. He got to know personally far away lands such as Syria, Palestine, and Egypt. He had much time to visit, to talk, to listen about religion and about philosophy.

For with his newly gained wealth and prestige, Mohammed pursued his consuming desire. He was constantly seeking for something that would satisfy his inner man. He was a thirsting man. Oh, if only someone could have met him and have given him the real truth!

He knew the Jews and Christians of his day.

The Jews had ample opportunity to win young Mohammed to the Jewish faith, to the true God, to the Ten Commandments. Though the contacts were many, this was not done. Possibly the Jewish leaders did not feel that this youth would mean much to the world and they paid no attention to him.

The Christians also had many contacts with him. He probably sat in many of their services and listened to them. It could be that the inconsistency of their business practices and lives could not convince him to follow their religion.

He did not see a spirit or a power in either the Jews or the Christians to convince him. But his writings show that he was influenced by them. He calls Abraham his father like the Jews call him their father. The Koran includes a strange story of Mary and the birth of Jesus.

He often retired to a cave to meditate upon religion. One day he had a vision which changed his destiny. He decided he was a prophet sent from Allah. He considered himself one of six great prophets sent from Allah. He called Adam a prophet, which he was not. He called Noah a prophet, which he was. He called Abraham a prophet, Moses a prophet, and Jesus a prophet. Of himself he said, "I am the last of the great prophets."

It is possible to stay alone and fabricate your own ideas until you get way out into desolation spiritually, thinking you are right. People living today have themselves way out in some corner, into cults and error.

The Word of God is Truth! And we have had it from the beginning of time. Paul said that even if an angel from heaven preaches any other gospel, we are not to accept it (Gal. 1:8).

For after all, Satan himself can appear as an angel of light, as can his ministers (2 Cor. 11:14).

We cannot accept any private revelations. The revelation God gave is in the Bible. Eternal Life is in the Bible.

Mohammed's Revelations

Mohammed heard voices. They came to him, not once or twice, but over a period of twenty-three years. He claimed the angel Gabriel dictated the Koran to him word by word.

The Koran, according to Mohammed, annuls the Bible. He declared that the Bible was corrupted by both Jews and Christians and not reliable.

Mohammed said in the Koran that Gabriel transmitted Islam's teachings undefiled, unmatched, and uncreated. He said they existed in heaven from the beginning.

The Koran has 114 Suras, or chapters, and contains 77,639 words.

In the Sura, XCVIII:5-7, Mohammed taught that Christians, Jews, and idolators are the worst of all created beings — and that Moslem believers are the best of all created beings.

In the Sura IV:14,29; IV:84,101,104, Moham-med taught that love is not as important as obedience or submission.

The Koran strictly teaches its followers to love their own believers — but not disbelievers. It encourages Moslems to wage a war (JIHAD) against non-Moslems in the name of Islam.

To kill a non-Moslem is justifiable. What is not permitted is to kill a believer, unless by mistake, in which case blood money must be paid to the victim's family.

Mohammed made polygamy a way of life. He gave Moslems permission to have four wives, although he himself had ten wives. He said this was through special permission from Allah.

Incidentally, after Khadijah died, within a year Mohammed married three more wives. One had been the wife of his adopted son. Another was a Jewish woman. The third was a Coptic Christian. Mohammed certainly must have heard the Old and New Testament stories from these women. His Koran contains Bible stories terribly twisted.

Mohammedanism teaches that Satan does not affect man's relationship with Allah. Neither does the Adamic nature of the human transmit sin to its offspring. Mohammedanism teaches that man is born sinless, that man has a tendency to sin, however, he has the ability to rise above his sins.

It is not man's relationship with God as much as it is the believer's relationship with other believers that is of great significance.

Bloodshed: Way to Sell a New Religion

The first person Mohammed convinced of his new religion was his wife, Khadijah. His new-phew, Ali, was the second. Many Moslems today are named after this Ali who became a strong supporter of Mohammed and his ideas and was one of the first leaders of the new religion.

Mohammed had a difficult time teaching his new religion. He was persecuted and driven from his native Mecca to Medina. His flight is called hegira. He gathered his faithful around him and taught them that the only way to win the world to Allah was by force, with the sword.

The forceful overthrow of the government of Medina came in 622 AD, the same year he arrived. The city was converted to Islam — except for some Jews and a few Christians — and Mohammed became its ruler as well as its religious high priest.

The former camel driver turned prophet, priest, ruler, lawgiver, and judge, also became commander-in-chief of JIHAD's first armed forces. He attacked Mecca, defeated its army, destroyed its idols, and established the new religion of Islam.

Medina and Mecca, where it all started, are the most holy places of the confederation. As the Jews taught Mohammed to face Jerusalem to pray, he taught his followers to face Mecca to pray.

At the time of his death, Mohammed had united almost all Arabia politically and religiously under Moslem control. And he had turned his thoughts toward Persia and the world.

After his death, the enthusiasm of Mohammedanism began to rise in fanatical fury. Those near him were determined to carry on his cause. They captured area after area and planted the Crescent and the new religion of Islam.

Islam's leaders were fierce and uncompromising. To disobey them was to die.

In less than twenty-five years, Mohammed's followers had captured Persia, Syria, Palestine, and Egypt.

In less than seventy-five years, they had taken North Africa and had entered Europe through Spain. It was only by a miracle of God that Charles Martel defeated the Moslems at the Battle of Tours in 732 AD and stopped the progress of Mohammedanism in Europe.

Mohammedanism had become the dominant power of the Mediterranean world. Its realm of influence stretched from the Atlantic Ocean to the borders of China, encompassing all the great empires of past history.

During the 7th and 8th centuries, Islam moved westward into Central Asia. Irresistibly, century after century, it gained converts until most of Northern India had fallen before its sword. In the 15th and 16th centuries, Islam moved toward the Far East into Java, Sumatra, and many islands, including the Philippines.

All of the bloodshed was justifiable in the name of JIHAD. One of Islam's greatest leaders was Abu Bekr, who immediately followed Mohammed into leadership. He wrote to cities and countries of Arabia to become subservient to the new religion. He sent his followers into Syria to take out of the hands of the infidels the powers of state and religion. He told them, "And I would have you know that fighting for religion is an act of obedience to Allah."

The first Syrian city he conquered was Bosra. A man named Romanus was the leader of this city. The invaders caused him to say publicly these words, "I deny Him that was crucified, and whosoever worships him. I choose God for my Lord, Islam for my faith, Mecca for my temple, the Moslems for my brethren, and Mohammed for my prophet." (*The History of Nations*, by Lodge, page 418.)

Islam and Iran

When the Islamic religion invaded Iran, possibly the hardest persecuted were the Zoroastrians. When Islam became the State religion, its leaders slowly persecuted the Christians and other dissenters. It assessed them extra taxes. It forbade Christians to make converts. It refused Christians the permission to display the Cross at all. Persecution varied by the provinces and also by the rulers over them.

In the early history of Iran, the Church had prospered under kings such as Sassiens from 224AD to 642AD. The city of Shush was the center of Christianity. But with the coming of Mohammedanism, they were overwhelmed. By the time Genghis Khan, the Mongol monarch, marched across Iran in the middle 1200s, the Church was almost eliminated. The remnant fled to the mountains in western Iran. And the Church never knew strength again in that land.

Christianity Today in Iran

The largest professing group of Christians in Iran are the Armenians, possibly one hundred sixty thousand strong. These Armenians date back to the first century. They are a closely knit people who mostly intermarry. The book, *Christians in Persia*, states that in the year 1624 Shah Abbas passed a law that any Christian who became a Moslem could claim the property of any of his relatives back to at least four generations. It was said that possibly fifty thousand Christians renounced their faith in order to get property. Very few of these were Armenians.

Holy Places: Price of Non-Evangelism

Maybe the strongest thing we could say in this book is that the Jews had ample time and place to win Mohammed to their religion. In this they failed.

What they did not know was that the day would come when a Mohammedan mosque, the Mosque of Omar, would be erected on the very sight of Solomon's Temple. Rather than the prayers of the Jews being heard in that place, there would be prayers to Allah.

To the Jews, one of the most sacred spots on the earth is Hebron where Abraham lived, where the angels talked to him at his front door, and the cave of Machpelah where he is buried. Five patriarchs are buried in the cave at Hebron. But rather than its being a Jewish place of reverence, respect, and prayer, it has a Mohammedan mosque over it. Mohammedan prayers are screamed from the minaret towers several times a day.

What a tremendous reminder that if we do not win sinners to Christ, they will turn and destroy us. I have so often wondered what a different world we would have if some Christian in Austria had won Adolf Hitler to the Lord Jesus Christ. It could have saved 50 million people from destruction by the war! When we do not evangelize, we suffer the consequences of it. Any person you refuse to win to Christ can become your adversary.

Christians, too, had ample opportunity to win Mohammed. He met many of them in his travels across the Fertile Crescent passing through Syria and Palestine into Egypt. He must have known much about Christianity. He saw its large churches, met its dignitaries, yet no one converted him.

One result is that possibly the most sacred place on earth for the Christians — the top of Mount Calvary — is a Moslem cemetery.

Few Christians ever walk on that mountain. Steel gates, a big chain, and a lock keep them out. I have been up there several times, especially when I lived in Israel. I always gave the porter a gift, but even then there is a reluctance to admit an "infidel" to walk around those Moslem graves on Mount Calvary.

As one looks up at the face of Golgotha (meaning skull) and sees the indentations in the side of the rock which must have given it its name, immediately below he sees an Arab bus station.

From early morning to late evening animals cry as they are carried in and out, all kinds of freight is continuously handled, busses toot their horns, people scream and yell in front of Calvary making it one of the most active spots of humanity I have seen — and all this within ten feet of Golgotha where the Son of God gave His life to save the entire human race.

This bus station was not built in 1950, when I first began visiting the Holy Land. I wrote a letter to the mayor of Jerusalem, whom I knew when we lived there, asking him if it could be moved. He answered that the Moslem population would never permit such a thing.

What a price Christendom paid for not evangelizing everyone, everywhere with the Gospel of the Lord Jesus Christ! Today the

Mohammedan religion is approaching the one billion mark in followers.

The most populous Moslem nation in the world is Indonesia with over 100 million Moslems. Africa has 225 million, Europe has 20 million, and the United States has a possible 2 million Moslems. Russia has 54 million Moslems within its borders.

World Dominance

A Moslem leader recently said, "Unless we win London to Islam, we will fail to win the whole of the western world."

The whole of the western world is the ambition of the Moslem world.

In London there are some three hundred thousand Moslems today. They have thirty-three mosques scattered over the city. The Central Mosque and Islamic Cultural Center was built recently in Regents Park in London at a cost of $7.5 million.

Is it possible that the nations of the West have not yet begun to realize the confrontation that is before them? For JIHAD is the religious "duty" of the world's Moslems.

JIHAD: Holy War

Chapter 9
JIHAD and
the Crusades

Possibly the greatest time of slaughter during the conflict between the Crescent and the Cross was during the crusades when the Christians of Europe undertook military expeditions to recover the Holy Land from the Moslems.

They began in 1096 AD when Peter the Hermit moved possibly six million people in Europe into a fury, begging them to regain the holy places in Palestine to the Christians.

He personally led a crusade of men — who history relates were unprepared in training and arms, neither did they understand the difficulties and dangers of their conflict. Most perished enroute from exposure, hunger, disease, and war.

A decisive battle was the famous battle at the Horns of Hattin fought in 1187 A.D. The Crusaders had passed from the Mediterranean to Nazareth where they settled. Their strategy was to go over the Galilean hills to the Sea of Galilee and engage the Moslem sultan, Saladin, and his forces in conflict.

King Guy of England had twenty thousand soldiers and one hundred twenty knights. What he did not realize was, the Moslems had an army of eighty thousand awaiting him. Many died in the bloody slaughter that ensued.

The crusades continued from the end of the 11th century until the end of the 13th century. Millions suffered and died on both sides. Both sides claimed Abraham as their father and that they believed in the one true God.

It is one of the darkest pictures of human history.

Chapter 10
Twentieth Century JIHAD

Upon the entry of Islam into the world in the 6th century, the deserts rang out with a new cry: "JIHAD! Holy War!"

This new religion on the world's scene would stand up angrily before the old religions. It would demand its place in the forum of religions.

It would differ greatly from Buddhism, already a thousand years old. There could be no idols or multiplicity of gods. In fact, there could be only the one God as the Judeo-Christian religions believed.

This oft-repeated tenet of the Moslem faith makes it clear: There is no god but Allah; Mohammed is his prophet.

This newest of religions would bring a new world. It would use the sword to convert tribes, nations, and empires to Islam.

The hot sands of Arabia would become the bloody sands of religious fanaticism. Synagogues of the Jews and churches of the Christians would be turned into mosques.

Today, in the 20th century, the backbones of Western statesmen are trembling as persistant and prophetic voices are heard coming from the burning sands of the deserts of ancient Persia, Babylon, Elam, Ur and Shushan.

They are crying to the Moslem world, "WE WANT JIHAD! WE WANT HOLY WAR!"

Iran and JIHAD

The crisis in the nation of Iran where sixty-three hostages were taken from the American Embassy in Tehran (ten were later released) by militants and radicals was not a political maneuver. It was not an accidental situation.

It was spiritual! It is prophetical!

Modern Iran with its population of thirty-five million people and its relation with ancient Persia has a remarkable relationship to prophetic destiny — much of which remains to be fulfilled.

Shah Mohammad Reza Pahlevi, like Esther's husband before him, knew how to hold sumptuous festivities. In 1971 he held a wild $100 million celebration to commemorate twenty-five hundred years of recorded history. This man's father had changed the name from Persia to Iran in 1935.

However, as we have seen, the true story of Iran actually dates back four thousand years. The people of Iran can measure their times from Noahs' Ark to the antichrist.

Not many nations have survived such millennia. Iran, or Elam as it was known in the early days, as a people went through the terror of the Tower of Babel when in one night all the languages and dialects of the world were created by God. They were a people in the days of Peleg when God divided the continents, sub-continents, islands, and scattered the seas.

It is easy to measure the time of their lineage from Noah's son, Elam.

The Bible records ten generations from Noah to Abraham. (Genesis 11). Matthew 1:17 specifically states that from Abraham to David was fourteen generations — from David to Babylon was fourteen generations — and from Babylon to Christ was fourteen generations. This totals fifty-two generations. If a generation is forty years, as the Bible says, this equals two thousand and eighty years.

And, of course, today's calendar counts time from Christ until now in a reasonably close proximity. Therefore, the roots of Iran can be traced four thousand years.

We have also traced the religious roots of Iran and have seen how Islam became the principle ruling religion of this Moslem state.

A House Divided

It should be realized not all Arabs are Moslems. Many evangelical Arabs belong to Baptist, Methodist, Presbyterian, and Full Gospel churches.

The Coptic Church is one of the oldest churches in the world, dating back before the birth of Mohammadism.

We have already mentioned the Armenian Arabs who have held fast to their Christian beliefs through many centuries of persecution.

Druids are scattered throughout the Arab world, but they are not Moslems.

Turkey has a large number of Kurds. As does Iran.

The Arabs who are Moslems are divided into a number of sects.

The Summa, also known as Sunni, make up approximately ninety percent of all Moslems. This largest group is the more conservative.

The Shi'ites compose only about ten percent of the Moslem religion. They are the more militant.

The Shi'ites believe that the successors of Mohammed by heredity assume spiritual and political rulership.

The Shi'ites teach that the religious leaders have supernatural wisdom not available to other men. They teach that these religious leaders may make decisions above the political leaders and that they must be obeyed.

Anwar Sadat of Egypt is a Sunni, of the conservative sect.

Ayatullah Ruhollah Khomeini is a Shi'ite, of the militant group.

Shi'ite Mobilizer for JIHAD

In 1963 Iran was swept by riots stirred up by powerful Islamic Shi'ite leaders. (In Iran ninety percent of its Moslems are Shi'ites.) These riots protested Shah Mohammad Reza Pahlevi's Western ways, calling him a traitor to Islam.

The Shah put down the disturbances and arrested one of its religious instigators — Ayatollah Ruhollah Khomeini.

Khomeini was exiled first to Turkey and then to Iraq. But he could not be silenced. He continued to preach against the idolatrous Shah — and for "a new nation of Islam."

His philosophy is summed up in this statement to reporters, "Islam means everything . . . Islam contains everything. Islam includes everything. Islam is everything."

And Islam, as we have seen, demands JIHAD. Even as Khomeini sat in exile, he sowed seeds of Holy War in Iran.

He constantly cried out that the Shah and his U.S. ties must go.

The major reason for the downfall of the Shah was his opposition to his own religion — Shi'ite Mohammedanism — and to Ayatollah Khomeini. When it became apparent that Khomeini's followers were everywhere displaying the Ayatollah's picture, the Shah put pressure on the government of Iraq to put him out of the country.

Khomeini fled to a small village outside Paris in October 1978. And from there he broadcast his message against Western theology, taking advantage of Western technology's most modern means of communication.

He talked to the Western press.

He sent his messages into the streets of Tehran by means of cassette tapes, often sold by sidewalk vendors. These were played in the mosques and in the homes of the people — every day gathering more power and strength for Khomeini and his call for a return to pure Islamic ways and goals.

He could pick up a telephone in Paris and his followers in Tehran would march in the streets.

He called for strikes, shut down banks and the postal service, closed factories, shops, and oil wells.

The Shah was powerless to stop it. On January 16, 1979, the Shah left the country and with it his ancestral throne ending one of the earth's oldest monarchies.

On February 1, 1979, the Imman Khomeini returned in triumph from France after fifteen years as a political exile. He was met by millions of jubilant Iranians shouting, "The holy one has come! He is the light of our lives!"

Khomeini assumed the political and religious leadership of the nation being designated as Iran's ruler for life.

Chapter 11
JIHAD
Against America

November 4, 1979 will go down in history as a day of infamy and shame.

Iran, the Imman, and Islam grabbed the attention of the world by attacking the U.S. Embassy in Tehran. It was besieged and captured.

A large number of people were inside the embassy doing business that day. No high American official was present. Sixty-three American hostages were taken. Ten were re-leased later. Fifty-three were held.

On the 156th day of the captivity of the American hostages, the United States had exhausted its patience and broke diplomatic relations with Iran. They had sought aid and assistance from every available group — the United Nations, the World Court, the Common Market nations of Europe. Nothing availed.

Most of the world does not even understand the type of war that is being waged.

Yet Khomeini made it very plain that this was JIHAD.

His cries were not heard across a sandy desert plain; they were carried around the world by the 20th century's sophisticated media.

Only Satan could have caused him to set out upon such a dangerous course at this time in history.

Operation Eagle Claw

The desert debacle of Friday, April 20, 1980, was called Eagle Claw by the Pentagon. It was given this name to hold its secret mission. It was under the direction of Colonel Charles Beckwith.

The American government decided to recapture the American Embassy in Tehran and to free the people who had been imprisoned at that time for over half a year.

The military rescue effort was aborted in the staging area in Iran's great salt desert 250 miles from the target in Tehran.

Terrible wind storms whipped up the desert sand in unbelievable fury. The men could not see where to go.

It ended with eight U.S. servicemen left dead on the burning sands surrounded by three disabled Sea Stallion helicopters and a great C-130 Hercules transport burned to a crisp.

I personally asked God why such a nation as America with the finest equipment on the face of this earth and the best fighting men on the face of this earth should fail in a mission such as this. I prayed desperately for an answer. It was not only for me — it was for the whole Western world.

Khomeini's Cries of JIHAD

"This is not a struggle between the United States and Iran," Khomeini declared. "It is a struggle between Islam and the infidels."

Here Khomeini is definitely saying this is not a political situation, but a religious one. All who are not Moslems are considered infidels.

"America is the mother of corruption," Khomeini stated in a speech.

Because of the strength of evangelism and Bibles being distributed from the United States, Khomeini considers this evangelical thrust as the one which gives birth to what he considers corruption.

"The United States is Enemy Number One of humanity," Khomeini said in a radio broadcast.

Khomeini makes statements like this because ninety percent of all missionary dollars going out around the world to convert people to the Lord Jesus Christ, come from the United States. Therefore he openly declares that we are a greater threat to him than the Russians on his north who are infidels and killers, as they have shown in Afghanistan.

"Why should we be afraid?" Khomeini says of any American attempt to use force. "We consider martyrdom a great honor."

These people are the ultimate fanatics and are possessed with a desire to militantly subdue nations and take them from the true life in Christ.

In a radio broadcast, Khomeini screamed for the entire Islamic world to join him. "Join us in this struggle between the infidel and Islam!"

"All Moslems should join us," he said, "because if this revolution fails, the East and Moslem countries will be destroyed as a result."

"This is not a struggle between the U.S. and Iran," he said in another speech. "It is a struggle between Islam and blasphemy."

It is very possible the people of the Western world have not until this point identified the titanic struggle in the breast of the Moslem to destroy Christianity and Judaism off the face of the earth.

One has to go back into the middle ages and carefully study the terrible battles between the crusaders and the Moslems to understand this fury.

One finds it difficult to see how the flames of hatred and revolution could burn for fourteen hundred years unless they are satanic in origin.

Khomeini's inflammatory statements set off a rash of incidents around the world.

Strangest of all and perhaps the most likely to

shock the Moslem world, five hundred terrorists dressed as pilgrims attacked Islam's holiest shrine, the Grand Mosque in Mecca. A radical Moslem cult sought recognition of its leader as the Islamic Messiah. (Moslems believe a secret Imman will one day appear. There will be, according to Moslem belief, no more prophets. Mohammed was the last. But directly under the prophets are the Immans.)

Government troops reclaimed the mosque, but not before several days' fighting and several men dying.

Khomeini found a way to blame the U.S. and Israel for the attack.

An enraged mob attacked the U.S. Embassy in Pakistan. They burned our magnificent government building; two Americans were killed. Pakistani government troops rescued 100 Americans who had been trapped inside the burning building for hours.

The U.S. Consulate building in Izmir, Turkey was stoned and windows were broken.

In Dacca, Bangladesh, mobs shouted, "Down with American imperialism!"

In Calcutta, India our President was burned in effigy.

Khomeini was hoping to start the real JIHAD. Had he been successful, there would have been the greatest religious battle the world had ever known.

Were we a first-class nation or not?

The Lord spoke back to me the same Friday that President Carter made his speech relating to the aborted raid.

God said, "I stopped the Americans in the desert before reaching the city, because had they done so, there would have been more bloodshed than has ever been imagined."

I trembled to think of this. I thought of how it might have triggered the confrontation with Russia — and how it could have been a world war which would have aroused the whole of the Arab world with a JIHAD such as history has no record of.

God gave the Russian world further opportunity to seek His face, repent of their sins, and ask His blessings upon their lives.

Iran with its Moslem fanatics held at bay the

whole Western world refusing to obey international law and begging the Arab states to refuse oil to the industrial nations of the world, which could bring the most chaotic condition this world has ever known.

Chapter 12
JIHAD: In Alliance with Infidels

We have dealt with Iran's long past, and somewhat with its present. We will deal now with its future.

As a nation, Iran is one of the oldest among mankind. How many nations can trace their existence as a people back to the flood?

Israel, as a people, can trace their existence back to Abraham — ten generations after the flood.

To be able to clearly identify the people of Iran from the time of Noah and the flood, through its famous world empire — the Persian Empire — and through its ultimate destiny is unparalleled as far as I am able to ascertain.

The Bible is the only source from which to derive this information.

We will see now what the Bible has to say about Iran's future.

A Land Desolated

The entire world knows that for two thousand years the land of Israel has been a desolate piece of property.

What brought about the desolation of the "Promised Land"?

Abraham came up out of Ur of the Chaldees as God's solitary prophet leaving the sin, the idolatry, and the paganism behind. He was to go to the land of Canaan to worship Jehovah and through his seed to bring the world a Savior.

When God called Abram out of Ur, He spoke to him about a promised seed and a promised land.

God said, *"Get thee out of thy country, and from thy kindred, and from thy father's house, unto a land that I will shew thee. And I will make of thee a great nation, and I will bless thee . . ."* (Gen. 12:1,2).

Later, God told Abraham how long this land would belong to his seed. *"For all the land which thou seest, to thee will I give it, and to thy seed forever"* (Gen. 13:15).

God specifically laid out the location of the land (Gen. 15:18-21) *"In the same day the LORD made a covenant with Abram, saying, Unto thy seed have I given this land, from the river of Egypt unto the great river, the river Euphrates: The Kenites, and the Kenizzites, and the Kadmonites, And the Hittites, and the Perrizzites, and the Rephaim, And the Amorites, and the Canaanites, and the Girgashites, and the Jebusites."*

God made a covenant with this people through whom He would bring a Savior to all men. He promised to bless them.

Moses was very careful to tell the people of Israel, speaking with the voice of God, the blessings that were theirs if they would remember God and His precepts — and the cursings they would suffer if they did not (Deut 28).

Israel forgot God. They forgot His sabbaths. They forgot His commandments. They forgot all the things God had done for them. So the Word of God in Deuteronomy 28 was fulfilled.

The rising power of empire overwhelmed them and they were taken into Babylonian captivity for over seventy years.

A remnant returned — some say one-sixth — to rebuild Jerusalem. But it was never the same as it had been in the days of David.

The prophets foretold that the peoples of Israel would wander and be dispersed among the heathen. And that as a result, their land would be desolate.

It has been estimated that at the beginning of the Christian era four million Jews lived in various parts of Europe, Asia, and Africa while seven hundred thousand lived in their own land.

The destruction of Jerusalem by Titus in 70 AD brought about the final scattering of the Jews.

When Israel followed God and occupied the land He gave them, the land showed forth His blessing. It was even called a land of milk and honey.

But when the rightful heirs were disobedient, or were gone all together, the land bore the shame of barrenness. It would never produce for anyone but its rightful owners.

A Land Revived

Ezekiel, the prophet of God, is a source of information relative to the last days of the "dispensation of grace."

In Ezekiel 36, he prophesied exactly how the land of Israel would be revived.

God Himself speaks to mountains! He requires them to change from a desolate place into a fruitful place!

Ezekiel was commanded of God to prophesy relative to the endtime saying that the mountains would shoot forth their branches — that they would yield their fruit to the people of Israel (v. 8).

Ezekiel prophesied that the land would again be tilled and sown (v. 9).

Ezekiel says that God will multiply man and beast; and they shall increase and bring fruit.

Then God, through the prophet Ezekiel, says, *"I will settle you after your old estates, and will do better unto you than at your beginnings: and ye shall know that I am the Lord"* (v. 11).

Through the centuries the earth of the Promised Land has been covered with blood many times. The Crusaders fought violently there to redeem Jerusalem for the Christians. Every major empire in history played its part there. The Roman empire devastated the land. And it has been devastated many times since.

For four hundred years the Turks ruled the land. They even put a tax on trees to where people cut down their trees in order not to pay tax. And the land became exceedingly desolate.

But in my lifetime — in the past twenty-five to thirty years — God changed the land.

He brought back rain upon the soil. He caused millions of trees to be planted. The entire land today has had a rebirth from barrenness to fruitfulness.

Some of the most delicious fruit I have tasted in the world — and I have lived and ministered in over 100 countries — grows on the hillsides of Israel.

The world has watched while Ezekiel's

twenty-five hundred year old prophecy of a land's reviving came true.

The Revival of a Nation

In the very next chapter, chapter 37, God calls the prophet Ezekiel to prophesy relative to a nation.

He had prophesied to the waste places. He had prophesied to the desolate ground. And now the Spirit of God takes him to a valley full of dry bones.

God asked the prophet, "Son of man, can these bones live?"

Ezekiel was so astounded at the sight of the bleached bones in the desert, that he had to say, "O Lord God, thou knowest."

In all the universe, God was the only one who believed that He could gather men from more than one hundred countries of the world and cause them to fit into one body to become a strong nation.

Listen to what God told Ezekiel to prophesy to the scattered bones, *"Prophesy unto these bones, and say unto them, O ye dry bones, hear the word of the Lord. Thus saith the Lord God unto these bones; Behold, I will cause breath to enter into you, and ye shall live . . . and ye shall know that I am the Lord"* (vv. 4,5).

Ezekiel obeyed God. He prophesied to the bones. Then he watched them come together, stand upon their feet, and become an exceeding great army (v. 10).

Then God told Ezekiel who the bones were: *"Then he said unto me, Son of man, these bones are the whole house of Israel"* (v. 11).

God said, *"I will take the children of Israel from among the heathen, whither they be gone, and will gather them on every side, and bring them into their own land: And I will make them one nation in the land upon the mountains of Israel..."* (vv. 21, 22).

In our lifetime, we have seen the Israeli people come from the four corners of the earth. We have watched them assemble themselves in their old places and build a nation with such vigor and passion that with less than four million of them, they could challenge one hundred million neighbors.

Incredible! Yet all knowledgeable observers agree this has already been accomplished and that this miracle has been performed in our times.

Again, the prophet Ezekiel in two successive chapters has met the test of a true prophet — his prophecies have been fulfilled.

Now we come to the next two chapters of Ezekiel — 38 and 39 — where we see one of the most astounding prophecies of history.

This next prophecy of Ezekiel has been written about — it has been much discussed — and it is very near completion. It gives the prophetic future of the ancient nation of Israel. But it also gives the prophetic future of the ancient nation of Iran — and the not-too-distant future of the USSR.

For the Sake of JIHAD! Iran Joins With Infidels

Again, Ezekiel is told to prophesy.

"Son of man, set they face against Gog, the land of Magog, the chief prince of Meshech and Tubal, and prophesy against him" (Ezek. 38:2).

We can identify to whom God refers by going back to Genesis chapter 10 where the generations of the sons of Noah are given. Japheth was one of Noah's three sons.

"The sons of Japheth; Gomer, and Magog, and Madai, and Javan, and Tubal, and Meshech, and Tiras" (Gen. 10:2).

Magog, Tubal, and Meshech were grandsons of Noah. They settled north of the Black Sea and east. This is the land Ezekiel 38:2 names.

Most teachers on Bible prophecy clearly identify the combination of Soviet alliances to be these people. Moscow, in the west, and Tobolsk, in the east, of the Soviet Union are clearly recognizable.

What does Ezekiel prophesy to them?

"After many days thou shalt be visited: in the latter years thou shalt come into the land that is brought back from the sword, and is gathered out of many people, against the mountains of Israel, which have been always waste: but it is brought forth out of the nations, and they shall dwell safely all of them" (v. 8).

God identifies a time — in the latter years.

In the latter years, northern lands shall come down upon Israel, a people brought back from the sword. Israel — a persecuted people for two thousand years — would be attacked from the north in their own land where they had come to dwell in safety.

"Thou shalt ascend and come like a storm, thou shalt be like a cloud to cover the land, thou, and all thy bands, and many people with thee" (v. 9).

These people from the north shall come possibly in a larger military force than the world has ever before witnessed.

". . . thou shalt think an evil thought: And thou shalt say, I will go up to the land of unwalled villages; I will go to them that are at rest, that dwell safely, all of them dwelling without walls, and having neither bars nor gates" (v. 11).

Such a thing was unheard of in the time Ezekiel wrote this. There were no such cities. There were no such towns. All towns had walls around them to protect the residents from wild beasts and hostile armies. They all had gates. They all had bars.

This was a prophecy that would not be understood by the people in Ezekiel's day, six hundred years before the Lord Jesus Christ was born.

They will come for a spoil. Read the 38th and 39th chapters of Ezekiel for the complete picture of a war before it is fought.

Now, let's go back a bit. The 9th verse said to Russia, *"all thy bands and many people with thee."*

Who will come down with Russia against Israel?

Verses 5 and 6 name the allies. The first one named is Persia.

"Persia, Ethiopia, and Libya with them; all of them with shield and helmet" (v. 5).

Persia — modern Iran.

Ethiopia — North Africa.

Libya — Eastern and North Africa, or it could be an area south of Kush in the area of Syria and Iran.

Other allies are mentioned in verse 6 — but the ones we have named would know the meaning of JIHAD.

The JIHAD! The Holy War! And Persia will be leading the way in this battle.

Iran is destined to join the atheists — the communists of Russia — to come against Israel.

Only in madness would this thing be conceived. Only in anger of the deepest sort could it be brought forth.

These people who believe that Allah is the one true god, will join with infidels of Russia who do not believe in God, to come against Israel whose father is Abraham.

The World News

No doubt the world news in the near future will give an amazing broadcast like this:

"Ladies and gentlemen: We have very bad news to report. Millions of people have joined with the Soviet Union in a march upon Israel. Israel has moved into the oil reserve regions of Arabia and has captured them. Israel must be stopped, otherwise Israel will control the entire world. Therefore the united armies of the Socialist Republics with allies which include most of the Arab states, with the exception of Egypt and Jordan, are marching against Israel tonight.

"Ladies and gentlemen, by tomorrow morning, there will be no Israel. So many of these people are marching south, it seems like a cloud. The sun is hardly visible with the dust that rises from this mightiest army of mankind. This is Israel's last night on this earth as the nation of Israel. Tomorrow morning it will be no more."

The Next Day

The following day the world news report will be as follows:

"Ladies and gentlemen: There is a surprise in world news. Yesterday it was forecast that today Israel would no longer be a nation. But from our reporters in that area, we have learned that a strange phenomenon has taken place.

"Israel is very much alive! But Russia and its allies are dead!

"At this moment we are not able to explain this. We are only able to say that very strong radio and television stations out of Jerusalem are inviting the entire world to come to Israel. Millions are dead. Israeli officials are asking visitors to bring a shovel. Anyone can keep all the riches they may find on any body they will bury. Officials have predicted it will take seven months to bury all the dead (Ezek. 39:12). Long live Israel!"

That is what a broadcast may sound like after it happens.

God forecast it twenty-six hundred years before it happens. And just as certainly as Ezekiel chapter 36 came to pass regarding the restoration of the land — and just as certainly as Ezekiel chapter 37 came to pass regarding the coming together of the peoples from dispersion — Ezekiel 38 and 39 will come to pass in full.

God foretold that "in the latter days" those who have fought against Him and denied Him, and those who agree to walk with them, will die on the vast plains of Megiddo in northern Israel.

God Himself will fight against those people who come against Israel, *"I will plead against him with pestilence and with blood; and I will rain upon him, and upon his bands, and upon the many people that are with him, an overflowing rain, and great hailstones, fire, and brimstone. Thus will I magnify myself and sanctify* (honor) *myself; and I will be known in the eyes of many nations, and they shall know that I am the Lord"* (v. 22, 23).

"And it shall come to pass in that day, that I will give unto Gog a place there of graves in Israel, the valley of the passengers on the east of the sea: and it shall stop the noses of the passengers: and there shall they bury Gog and all his multitude: and they shall call it The valley of Hamongog. And seven months shall the house of Israel be burying of them, that they may cleanse the land.

"Yea, all the people of the land shall bury them; and it shall be to them a renown the day that I shall be glorified, saith the Lord God.

"And they shall sever out men of continual employment, passing through the land to bury with the passengers those that remain upon the face of the earth, to cleanse it: after the end of seven months shall they search.

"And the passengers that pass through the land, when any seeth a man's bone, then shall he set up a sign by it, till the buriers have buried it in the valley of Hamongog" (Ezek. 39:11-15).

God sums up the situation in Ezekiel 39:28,29. *"Then shall they know that I am the Lord their God, which caused them to be led into captivity among the heathen: but I have gathered them unto their own land, and have left none of them any more there. Neither will I hide my face any more from them: for I have poured out my spirit upon the house of Israel, saith the Lord God."*

Iran, that nation which had the witness of God in the miracle of the Jews salvation during the years of their Jewish queen, Esther . . .

Iran, that nation which had the witness of the wise men . . .

Iran, that nation which had the witness of the people who were at the first outpouring of the Holy Spirit and the birth of the Church . . .

Iran, who despite all that, chose Islam and JIHAD, will find devastation and desolation on the plains of Megiddo.

Chapter 13
The Final JIHAD

Our earth has known great wars. It has known much bloodshed. But after the final war, the day of peace will come.

Closing out the great tribulation, Jesus Christ will return to personally fight against the anti-christ and his armies to destroy them.

A prophecy we have already looked at foretold it. One of the most outstanding prophecies of the entire Bible is the vision the first world empire builder saw. Let's look at it again. This time paying particular attention to the last part.

"Thou, O king, sawest, and behold a great image. This great image, whose brightness was excellent, stood before thee; and the form thereof was terrible.

"This image's head was of fine gold, his breast and his arms of silver, his belly and his thighs of brass, His legs of iron, his feet part of iron and part of clay.

"Thou sawest till that a stone was cut out without hands, which smote the image upon his feet that were of iron and clay, and brake them to pieces" (Dan. 2:31-34).

This is the final JIHAD.

A Stone would be cut without hands from the mountain. This Stone is Jesus. He is the Rock of Ages. He is the Smiting Stone. He is the Cornerstone of all civilization.

He was cut without hands. He was born of a virgin. He did not come to this earth as other men had come. He came as the Son of God to redeem the world from its sins. He was not promoted to a place of authority by any human instrument. He had no natural assistance in making him the King of kings and the Lord of lords. This Stone was cut without hands.

God says this Stone smote the image upon his feet which were of iron and clay and brake them to pieces.

Why his feet?

Because that's the time in history in which He strikes. The Stone without hands does not smite in the time of the gold, or the silver, or the brass. It smites in the last days of this world's empires.

The Stone strikes the ten-toed kingdom of the antichrist, which is very likely being brought into existence today through the Common Market countries of Europe.

This ten-nation confederacy will choose a fateful leader. That leader will befriend Israel and make a seven-year covenant with her after she has defeated Russia.

At the destruction of Russia as a world power, the next great power will be that of the Common Market countries of Europe. They will be the richest and most powerful of all nations. Already they exchange products with no import tariffs.

From these nations shall rise the antichrist. He will accuse God of all earth's problems. And forces under his leadership will war with God.

At that point, the Stone will smite the feet of this great image God spoke of so many years before.

"Then was the iron, the clay, the brass, the silver, and the gold, broken to pieces together, and became like the chaff of the summer threshingfloors; and the wind carried them away, that no place was found for them: and the stone that smote the image became a great mountain, and filled the whole earth" (Dan. 2:35).

How could the gold, the silver, the brass, the iron, and the clay be broken in pieces "together" when they are so many centuries apart?

What all these empires stood for still remains today. Each contributed its part to the chaotic conditions of today's world.

1. Babylon. It was in Babylon that the occult came into its power. Superstitions were born there. Babylon was the nesting place of spiritism, demonism, Satanism. The occult offspring of Babylon constitute one of the greatest problems in the world today. When that Stone which is cut without hands smites the image, Babylon will forever be defeated with all of its occult, sinister, nether-world teachings. All spiritism will completely die when Babylon is struck down by the Lord Jesus Christ.

2. The Persian Empire. The Persian empire represents indulgence. It represents every lust of the human flesh. It represents luxury at its highest. The very spirit of the Persian courts is in the world today, strongly anti-God, and destroying virtue. All the sins of the great Persian courts are on our highways and streets to this day. All the lewdness of our modern world has the spirit of Persia in it. And that Stone, when it comes, will smite and destroy these sins.

3. The Grecian Empire. Greece represents learning — philosophy — man without need for God — humanism is its strength. This empire remains with us today. It stalks down our university halls. It screams over the mass media saying that man is sufficient. He does not need God. He is acceptable in his own rights. Man can make a way for himself. When the Lord Jesus comes, He will smite this. The whole world shall know that God is God, and that Christ is the Savior of the world.

4. The Roman Empire. The Romans represented the people's government. "Let the will of the people be done," they said. The great power of Rome is with us today in the democracies of the world saying, "With government we can save ourselves. We can make laws to correct ourselves. Government is the answer."

I was in a Florida court room when the judge said, "In this room law is God."

I was astounded. I responded, "Judge, nowhere on this earth is law God." He did not listen.

Rome with all of its fantasies and assumed power failed. All human governments around the world have failed miserably. When that Stone smites them, they shall be broken in pieces.

The next few words of that prophecy are very significant. These empires — these achievements of man — shall become like the chaff of the summer threshingfloors. The wind will carry them away. No place will be found for them. When the Lord Jesus Christ shall rule over this earth for one thousand years, there will be no memories of these desolate empires which sought to rule man and the world.

God would have you realize that things of this world will pass away. The cults of Babylon, the luxury of Persia, the learning of the Greeks, the government of the Romans shall all be swept away. God says they will be like chaff. They will be as nothing. They will be blown away. The wind carries them away and no place is found for them. Forever they are gone from the memory of man.

The last line is wonderful!

The Stone that smote the image became a great mountain and filled the whole earth!

The Lord Jesus Christ shall become King of kings and Lord of lords! He shall become Master of all mankind.

The last JIHAD is when our Lord and Master becomes supreme upon the earth and destroys from it all forces of evil. He is the Conquering One who sets humanity free!

Revelation 17:14 describes that war: *"These shall make war with the Lamb, and the Lamb shall overcome them: for he is Lord of lords, and King of kings: and they that are with him are called, and chosen, and faithful."*

The final battle will be between the forces of antichrist against the power of the Lord Jesus Christ.

125

Details of the battle are already foretold. Its outcome is already decided. God revealed through His servant John that at the conclusion of the great bloodbath, Jesus has destroyed His enemies.

A multitude cries out!

"And I heard as it were the voice of a great multitude, and as the voice of many waters, and as the voice of mighty thunderings, saying, Alleluia: for the Lord God omnipotent reigneth " (Rev. 19:6).

There shall be a time when the Lord Jesus gathers His own redeemed unto Himself. They shall have a time of rejoicing when the Lord Jesus shall be forever united with His own.

"Let us be glad and rejoice, and give honour to him: for the marriage of the Lamb is come, and his wife hath made herself ready.

"And to her was granted that she should be arrayed in fine linen, clean and white: for the fine linen is the righteousness of saints.

"And he saith unto me, Write, Blessed are they which are called unto the marriage supper of the Lamb. And he saith unto me, These are the true sayings of God" (Rev. 19:7-9).

All those who are with the Lord shall be called together with Him.

"And I saw heaven opened, and behold a white horse; and he that sat upon him was called Faithful and True, and in righteousness he doth judge and make war.

"His eyes were as a flame of fire, and on his head were many crowns; and he had a name written, that no man knew, but he himself.

"And he was clothed with a vesture dipped in blood: and his name is called The Word of God.

"And the armies which were in heaven followed him upon white horses, clothed in fine linen, white and clean.

"And out of his mouth goeth a sharp sword, that with it he should smite the nations: and he shall rule them with a rod of iron: and he treadeth the winepress of the fierceness and wrath of Almighty God.

"And he hath on his vesture and on his thigh a name written, KING OF KINGS, AND LORD OF LORDS" (Rev. 19:11-16).

JIHAD

This is the consummation of all JIHAD!

There shall be no more wars. They shall cease.

There shall be no more tyranny. It shall cease.

There shall be no more anger. It shall cease.